ChordTime® Piano

Disney

LEVEL 2B

Arranged by Nancy and Randall Faber

T0079446

This book belongs to: _____

Production Coordinator: Jon Ophoff
Editor: Isabel Otero Bowen
Design and Illustration: Terpstra Design, San Francisco
Engraving: Dovetree Productions, Inc.

Disney Characters and Artwork © Disney

FABER
PIANO ADVENTURES®
HAL•LEONARD®

A NOTE TO TEACHERS

ChordTime® Piano Disney brings together contemporary and classic Disney hits arranged for the Level 2B pianist. In the words of Walt Disney, "There is more treasure in books than in all the pirates' loot on Treasure Island." This book offers musical treasure for piano students with blockbusters from *Beauty and the Beast, Moana, The Lion King, Tangled, The Little Mermaid,* and more.

Students develop confidence at the piano through mastery of scales and chords. The *ChordTime Piano* series explores these fundamentals in a setting of inspiring songs. Correlating to Level 2B of the Piano Adventures® method, the pieces are in the keys of C, G, and F major and feature I, IV, and V^7 chords with various accompaniment patterns. Each section of the book introduces a major key with scale and chord warm-ups for the pieces that follow.

ChordTime® Piano is part of the PreTime to BigTime Supplementary Piano Library arranged by Faber & Faber. The series allows students to enjoy a favorite style at their current level of study. ChordTime books are available in the following styles: *Popular, Classics, Favorites, Rock 'n Roll, Jazz & Blues, Ragtime & Marches, Hymns, Kids' Songs, Christmas, Jewish Favorites,* and the *Faber Studio Collection.*

Visit us at **PianoAdventures.com**.

Helpful Hints:

1. The chord warm-ups for a given key should be played daily before practicing the songs.
2. The student can be asked to identify the I, IV, and V7 chords in each song and write the correct chord symbol below the bass staff.
3. The student can be encouraged to identify any other chord that he or she is able to recognize and to label it accordingly (e.g., the occasional root position major or minor chord). It is helpful to encourage an atmosphere of discovery.

THE PRETIME TO BIGTIME PIANO LIBRARY

PreTime® Piano	=	Primer Level
PlayTime® Piano	=	Level 1
ShowTime® Piano	=	Level 2A
ChordTime® Piano	=	Level 2B
FunTime® Piano	=	Level 3A–3B
BigTime® Piano	=	Level 4 & above

ISBN 978-1-61677-700-5

Printed in U.S.A.

WARNING: The music, text, design, and graphics in this publication are protected by copyright law.
Any duplication is an infringement of U.S. copyright law.

FF3042

TABLE OF CONTENTS

I, IV, V^7 Chords in the Key of C

Supercalifragilisticexpialidocious (from *Mary Poppins*) 4

Belle (from *Beauty and the Beast*) 6

Be Our Guest (from *Beauty and the Beast*) 8

I've Got a Dream (from *Tangled*) 10

I, IV, V^7 Chords in the Key of G

I Just Can't Wait to Be King (from *The Lion King*) 13

Bella Notte (from *Lady and the Tramp*) 16

Circle of Life (from *The Lion King*) 18

I, IV, V^7 Chords in the Key of F

The Bare Necessities (from *The Jungle Book*) 21

Fathoms Below (from *The Little Mermaid*) 24

How Far I'll Go (from *Moana*) 26

Music Dictionary 29

Key of C

C Scale Warm-up: Play **H.A.** (Hands Alone), then **H.T.** (Hands Together).

f–p on repeat

Chord Warm-up:

mf I ("one") IV ("four") I IV I V^7 ("five-seven") I

Supercalifragilisticexpialidocious

from *Mary Poppins*

WHO SAID THIS?
You know, you can say it backwards,
which is Dociousaliexpiisticfragicalirupes —
but that's going a bit too far, don't you think?

Words and Music by
RICHARD M. SHERMAN
and ROBERT B. SHERMAN

Lively

p *mf*

5

mp Su - per - cal - i - frag - il - is - tic - ex - pi - al - i - do - cious!

© 1963 Wonderland Music Company, Inc.
Copyright Renewed.
All Rights Reserved. Used by Permission.

ANSWER: Mary Poppins

Belle

from *Beauty and the Beast*

WHO SAID THIS?
This is the day your dreams come true.

Music by ALAN MENKEN
Lyrics by HOWARD ASHMAN

Moderately fast

mf There goes the bak - er with his tray, like al - ways,
Look, there she goes. That girl is strange, no ques - tion.

5

the same old bread and rolls to sell. *p* *mf* Ev-'ry
Dazed and dis - tract - ed, can't you tell? Nev-er

cross 3 *over*

9

morn-ing just the same since the morn-ing that we came to this
part of an - y crowd. 'cause her head's stuck on some cloud. No de -

13

To Coda 𝄋

poor pro - vin - cial town. *(Good morn-ing, Belle.)* *mf*
ny - ing, she's a fun - ny girl that Belle.
cresc. *f*

turn 1 *under*

© 1991 Wonderland Music Company, Inc. and Walt Disney Music Company
All Rights Reserved. Used by Permission.

ANSWER: Gaston

Be Our Guest

from *Beauty and the Beast*

WHO SAID THIS?
And now, we invite you to relax.
Let us pull up a chair, as the dining
room proudly presents…your dinner.

Music by ALAN MENKEN
Words by HOWARD ASHMAN

© 1991 Wonderland Music Company, Inc. and Walt Disney Music Company
All Rights Reserved. Used by Permission.

ANSWER: Lumiere

I've Got a Dream

from *TANGLED*

WHO SAID THIS?
Something brought you here, Flynn Rider. Call it what you will—fate, destiny…

Music by ALAN MENKEN
Lyrics by GLENN SLATER

© 2010 Wonderland Music Company, Inc. and Walt Disney Music Company
All Rights Reserved. Used by Permission.

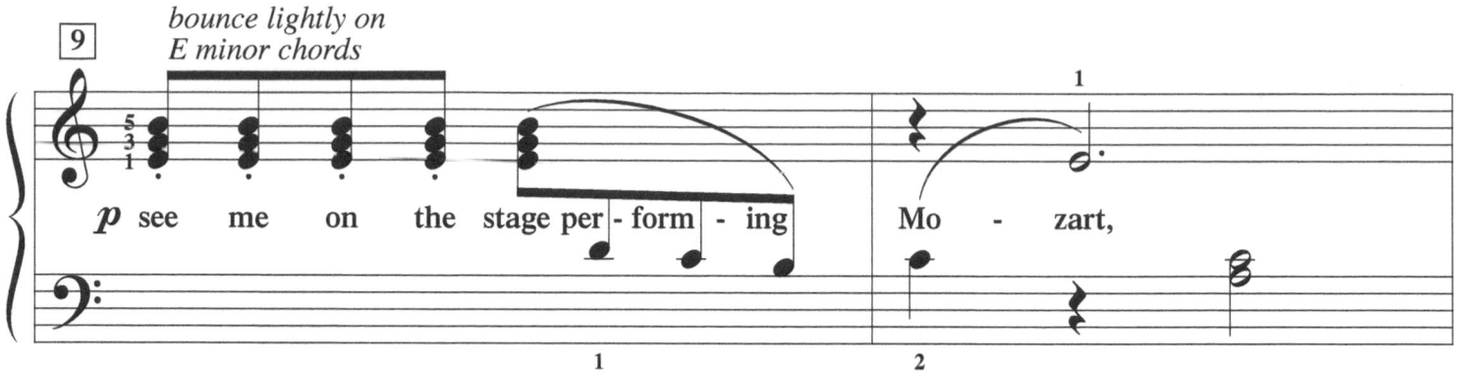

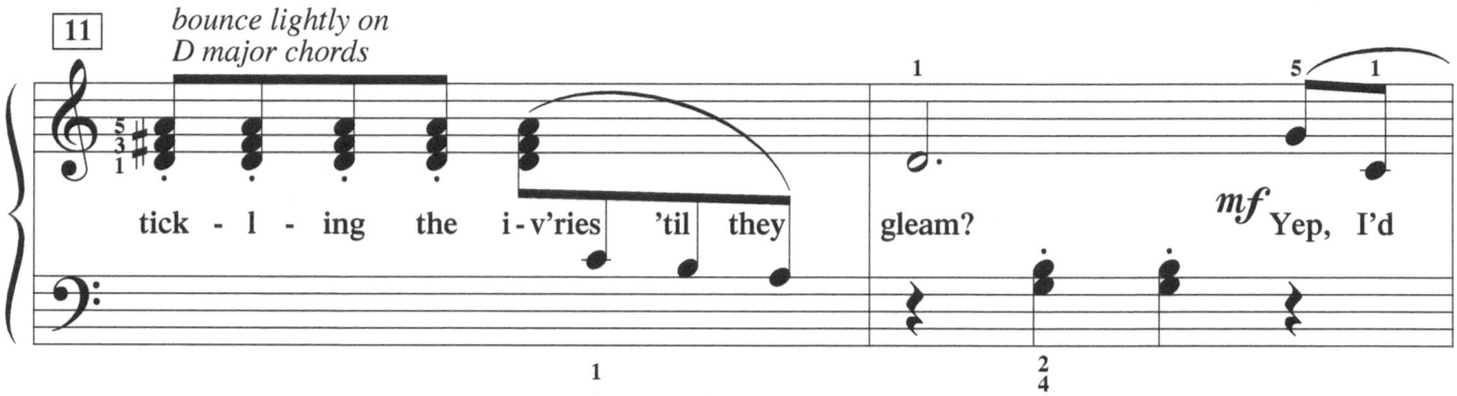

ANSWER: Rapunzel

17
shift
dream, he's got a dream. See, I
19
ain't as cruel and vi - cious as I seem. Though I
21
do like break - ing fe - murs, you could count me with the dream - ers. Like
23
ev - 'ry - bod - y else, I've got a dream. Yes,
25
turn under
way down deep in - side, I've got a dream.

Key of G

G Scale Warm-up: Play **H.A.** (Hands Alone), then **H.T.** (Hands Together).

f–p on repeat

Chord Warm-up:

mf I IV I V^7 I

I Just Can't Wait to Be King

from *The Lion King*

WHO SAID THIS?
My dad just showed me the whole kingdom. And I'm gonna rule it all.

Music by ELTON JOHN
Lyrics by TIM RICE

Lively

mf

I'm gon - na be a might - y king, so

en - e - mies be - ware! I've nev - er seen a

© 1994 Wonderland Music Company, Inc.
All Rights Reserved. Used by Permission.

ANSWER: Simba

6
king of beasts with quite so lit - tle hair. I'm
9
gon - na be the mane e - vent, like no king was be -
12
fore. I'm brush - ing up on look - ing down. I'm
15
work - ing on my roar. Thus far, a rath - er un - in - spir - ing
p
optional pedal

19
thing.
mf
f Oh, I just can't
shift to C chord
shift to D chord
22
wait to be
king!
Oh, I just can't
shift to G chord
26
wait to be
king!
30
(1 - 2 - 3 - 4 1 - 2 - 3 - 4)
f
8va

Bella Notte

from *Lady and the Tramp*

WHO SAID THIS?
Look, there's a great big hunk of world down there with no fence around it. Where two dogs can find adventure and excitement.

Music and Lyrics by
PEGGY LEE and
SONNY BURKE

© 1952 Walt Disney Music Company
Copyright Renewed.
All Rights Reserved. Used by Permission.

ANSWER: Tramp

Circle of Life

from *The Lion King*

WHO SAID THIS?
Everything the light touches is our kingdom.

Music by ELTON JOHN
Lyrics by TIM RICE

© 1994 Wonderland Music Company, Inc.
All Rights Reserved. Used by Permission.

9
far too much to take in here, more to find than can ev - er be
12
found. But the sun roll-ing high through the sap - phire sky keeps great and
mf
15
small on the end - less round. It's the cir - cle of
17
f life
lift
and it moves us

19
all
through de - spair and
lift
21
hope,
through faith and love.
mf
24
Till we find our
f
place,
on the path un -
27
wind - ing
p
in the
mf
cir - cle,
30
mp
the cir - cle of
life.
molto ritardando
f
8va

Key of F

F Scale Warm-up: Play **H.A.** (Hands Alone), then **H.T.** (Hands Together).

f–p on repeat

Chord Warm-up:

mf I IV I IV I V^7 I IV I

The Bare Necessities

from *The Jungle Book*

WHO SAID THIS?
Mowgli, don't you realize that you're a human?

Words and Music by
TERRY GILKYSON

Bright and snappy

mf Look for the bare ne - ces - si - ties, the

f

3

sim - ple bare ne - ces - si - ties, for - get a - bout your

© 1964 Wonderland Music Company, Inc.
Copyright Renewed.
All Rights Reserved. Used by Permission.

ANSWER: Baloo

6
wor - ries and your strife. I mean the bare ne -
10
ces - si - ties or Moth - er Na - ture's re - ci - pes that
13
bring the bare ne - ces - si - ties of life.
16
mp
Wher - ev - er I wan - der, wher - ev - er I

19
roam, I could-n't be fond - er of my big
23
shift
home. The bees are buzz - in' in the
cross over
26
tree to make some hon - ey just for me, the bare ne -
29
cross over
cessi - ties of life will come to you.
f

Fathoms Below

from *The Little Mermaid*

WHO SAID THIS?
Isn't this great? The salty sea air.
The wind blowing in your face.
Perfect day to be at sea!

Music by ALAN MENKEN
Lyrics by HOWARD ASHMAN

© 1988 Wonderland Music Company, Inc. and Walt Disney Music Company
All Rights Reserved. Used by Permission.

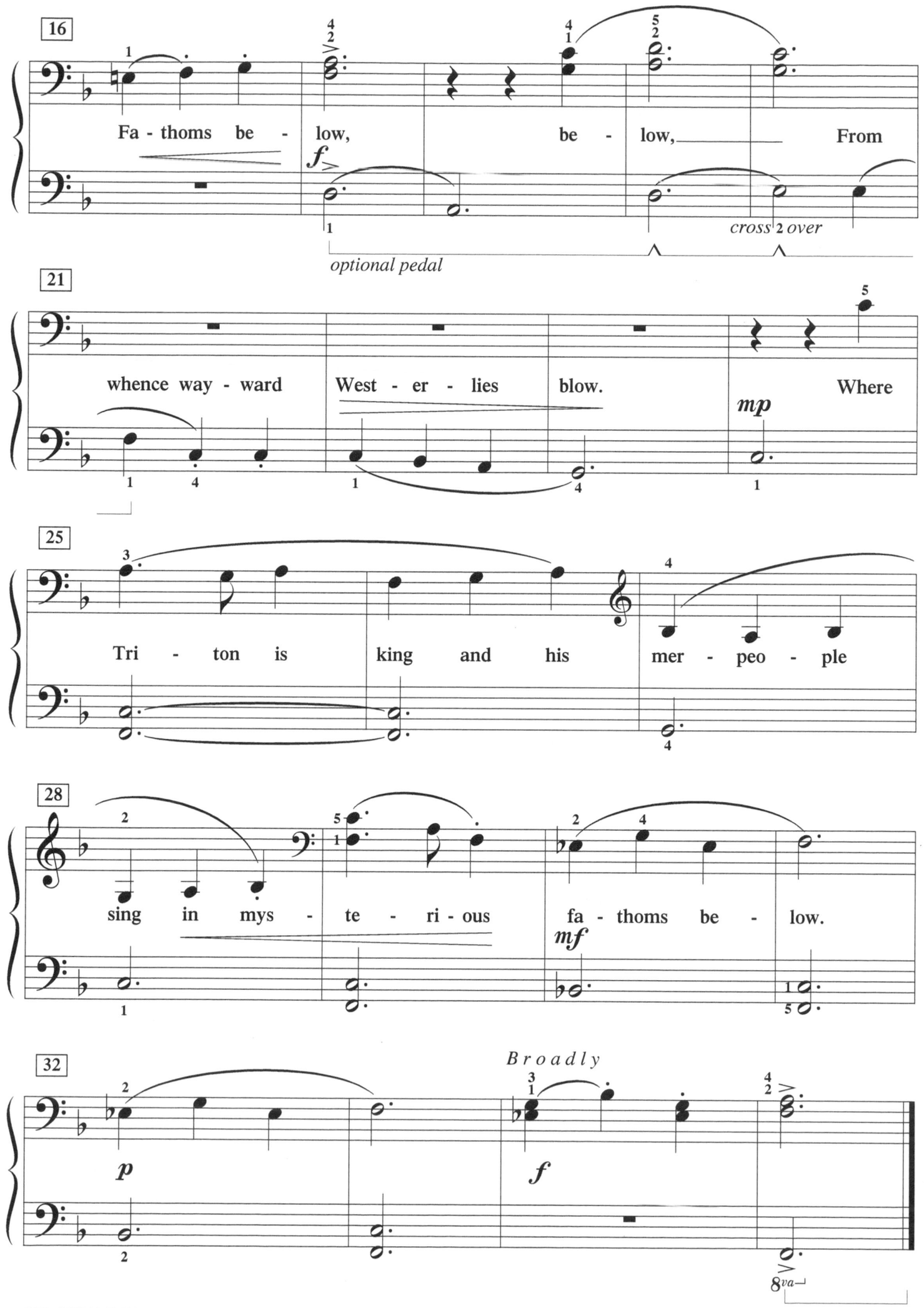
16
Fa - thoms be - low, be - low, From
f
optional pedal
cross over
21
whence way - ward West - er - lies blow. Where
mp
25
Tri - ton is king and his mer - peo - ple
28
sing in mys - te - ri - ous fa - thoms be - low.
mf
32
Broadly
p
f
8va

ANSWER: Eric

How Far I'll Go

from *Moana*

WHO SAID THIS?
You're measuring the stars.
Not giving the sky a high five.

Music and Lyrics by
LIN-MANUEL MIRANDA

© 2016 Walt Disney Music Company
All Rights Reserved. Used by Permission.

14
mf mat - ter how hard I try.
Ev - 'ry
mp
17
turn I take, ev - 'ry trail I track, ev - 'ry path I make, ev - 'ry
20
shift
road leads back to the place I know where I can not go, where I
cresc. poco a poco
shift
23
f long to be.
mf See the line where the sky meets the
26
(silently change to 1)
sea, it calls me, and no one

ANSWER: Maui

29
knows how far it goes.
32
If the wind in my sail on the sea stays be - hind
35
me, One day I'll know.
38
If I go, there's just no telling how far I'll
rit.
41
a tempo
mp
go.
p
rit.
pp
8va